A WEEKEND WITH RENOIR

A WEEKEND WITH
RENOIR

by Rosabianca Skira-Venturi

Rizzoli
NEW YORK

I have put on my little round hat (which I wear quite often, in fact), combed my white beard and put on my best navy-blue suit. I am wearing my favorite necktie, too. Surely you can see at once that I am a painter.

I am so pleased that you have come to spend the weekend with me, to hear me talk about myself and my friends—they are painters also. What I am about to tell you is my own true story—the story of my life and my work. You will have to step back with me into the past—before you were born, yes, but not so very long ago.

Let me take a last look in the mirror to make sure that everything is just right. This is how I see myself today: it is my *Self-Portrait.* I am sure that we will have a fine time together. But first, let me introduce myself to you. My name is Pierre-Auguste Renoir.

Renoir, Re-*noir*?

   In Renoir, there is the French word "noir," which means "black." But does that mean that my paintings are black and dark? Oh, no, certainly not! I am a painter who likes light colors: pink, green, yellow, blue. . . especially blue. Yet it is also true—I often say—that there should always be a little black to make the colors sing. Well, I say "sing," but perhaps that is not the right word. What I mean is that a touch of black helps the pinks, greens, yellows, and blues to stand out better against the light background of the picture.

When I was a young man, I dreamed of quitting my work as a china decorator to become an artist. I was fascinated by all of the painter's tools. If you ever walk along the lovely street in Paris called Quai Voltaire, do stop at No. 3. Here, facing the river Seine, is a fabulous art store, full of paint tubes of all sizes, with all the colors you could imagine, ready to be put onto canvas. Not to mention hundreds of different brushes, stretchers, boxes, easels, and even parasols . . . something to fulfill any artist's dream.

And what did I dream of? I dreamed of painting outdoors under the open sky, in the beautiful French countryside, capturing with my paints all of nature's colors. Does that sound like an easy thing to do? To tell the truth, it is not; but it began to seem possible to me, especially with the right equipment.

Palette Knife
(used to mix and apply paints)

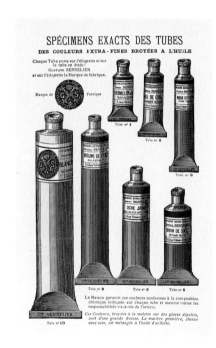

Paint Tubes

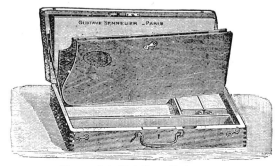

Box with Folding Palette
(a board on which to mix the paints)

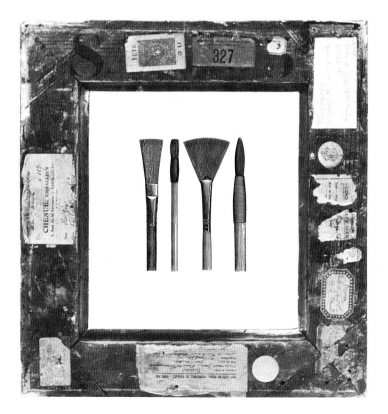

Wooden Stretcher

Like many of my painter friends, I paint in oil, using a brush to apply my colors onto a fairly fine cotton or linen canvas tacked onto a wooden frame called a stretcher. I do not draw on the canvas, but paint with light brushstrokes, making little swirls of green, then red, adding a bit of white, and so on. This is how I am able to do two things that matter a great deal to me:
—to capture the light, and
—to create movement.

Each of these needs the other if the painting is to be a success. To capture the light means to give life and movement to what I paint. (Animated cartoons, of course, had not yet been invented in my time!) But by the use of color, I am able to create the effects of light and movement.

I like to set up my easel outdoors and paint things as I see them: children playing on a swing, friends meeting in a café, a mother and her child, a woman after a swim feeling the warmth of the sun on her skin. Sometimes I make up little stories about them. I like to paint beautiful bouquets of flowers, too, full of colors and light—and the olive trees in the south of France, or the trees hanging over the banks of a river.

The red ball of the sun shines through the morning mist; the boats in the harbor look like blurred shadows. My friend Claude Monet painted this picture and called it *Impression, Sunrise*. He showed it at an art exhibition where, for the first time, people could see the new kind of painting we were doing. People who were used to old-fashioned painting were quite startled by our new, free style, which they called Impressionism. Some were angry—others just laughed at us. The artist Daumier made a cartoon, or drawing, of some of these stuffy people (*Les Bons Bour-*

geois, he called it) making fun of an Impressionist artist who is painting in a field.

LES BONS BOURGEOIS.

Some People Laughed at Us

But, though our critics did not mean it kindly, Impressionism was a good name for our new kind of painting. That is certainly what I like to do—to capture a moment of happiness and paint the impression it gives me. To paint this impression matters a lot to me and to my painter friends. So we did not mind being called Impressionists, which gradually came to mean painters who use their colors to try to give their impression of things: the impression of early morning, of a smile, of a graceful gesture.

One day I saw Aline—she was my fiancée then—looking at some fashion drawings (below). How charming she looked! I loved her red-gold hair, which almost hides her pretty face here. I took out a small canvas and painted this picture called *A Young Woman Reading an Illustrated Newspaper*. One of the illustrations she was looking at was quite a lot like my own drawing, *The Dressmaker* (at left), of a lovely young girl walking through Paris carrying a big basket.

The Plume of Smoke

My painter friends and I often take long walks, sometimes in the streets of the city, sometimes in the country, by the river. On our backs, we carry our boxes—they are heavy, full of tubes of paint, brushes, a palette (a board on which you mix the colors), the easel to hold the canvas—and a folding seat to sit on. To go outside of Paris, we take the train. Trains have not been running for very long.

In Paris, I like to look down from the tops of bridges at all the criss-crossed steel rails of the tracks, at the locomotives with their plumes of smoke, speeding their train cars full of passengers to the country. Today, I am not going very far with my painting equipment, just a little more than ten miles outside of Paris. I want to go and paint by the banks of the river Seine. I love that clear, calm river that flows through the beautiful French countryside and then winds through the heart of the city of Paris itself.

Charles-François Daubigny, a great painter, left us a fine picture of a train passing proudly over a bridge in a very amusing book: *The Traveller's Guide from Paris to the Sea*.

Photography, a very recent invention in my day, could also capture instants of nature, but, believe me, it was nothing like a painting. The photograph, on the opposite page, of the Boater's Dance Hall at Bougival is pleasant—but can it be compared to our paintings? Absolutely not. Just look at the small picture below, *The Seine at Argenteuil*. (Argenteuil is a town very near Bougival.) Though not as precise as the photograph, doesn't the painting tell you more about what the scene was really like? I painted it from the river bank, sitting right next to another painter, my friend Claude Monet.

Rowboat

Today I am not going to Argenteuil, but to the village of Bougival. It takes me barely twenty minutes to get there from Paris by train. I set up my easel to paint at a restaurant there called La Grenouillère. For me—and for my friends, too—it is a wonderful spot. The name, which comes from the French word for frog—"grenouille"—makes me think of a bunch of frogs hopping around and having fun. Strangely enough, I've never seen a single one there, but there must be some, for it is a very marshy area.

In the Warm Summer Air

La Grenouillère is the name of a riverside restaurant near Paris. It is well known to Parisians—and to foreigners as well. Crowds of people come here not only to eat, but also to swim, to row boats on the Seine, or just to have fun— but we come to paint. This charming spot has been pictured in many journals and guidebooks: for example, here is a print from a very popular newspaper called *The Illustrated World*. You can see young women wearing fashionable bathing suits and also, if you look carefully, men wearing the famous "boaters," a type of straw hat worn by those who row boats for work or for pleasure.

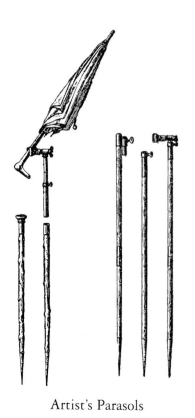

I have gone a little further, beyond Argenteuil (shown on the postcard above), to paint *La Grenouillère*. That is the name of a restaurant, yes, but also the title of many of the pictures I painted there with such enthusiasm! The boats, the dancing reflections on the water, and the colors— the brightly dressed people in the sunlight, the dappled shadows cast by the soft green leaves of the trees—how could I not be enchanted? But the sun is hot, too, and so I make some shade with my portable parasol: quite a handy thing for an outdoor painter like me.

Artist's Parasols

There is a sort of swimming club here, and the restaurant itself is on a floating raft. The little piece of land that connects it to the banks of the Seine is called Camembert. Such a funny name! I suppose it is called that because it is round, and cased in wood, like a delicious French cheese. Today, I feel like painting the boats—big and small, with and without sails—the rowboats, skiffs, and dinghies that go up and down the river.

Chatou (which is also on the right bank of the Seine) is another fashionable spot where wealthy people build fine country houses. I remember one afternoon—was it a Sunday?—when I painted *Oarsmen at Chatou*. My fiancée and friends posed for me. Aline is, as always, wonderfully graceful in every movement. My friends were very happy, as you can see, and the river is alive with skiffs, dinghies, and kayaks.

Outdoor Easel

The Seine is very busy here; there are also hundreds of barges and tugboats that pass by Bougival, often on their way to Argenteuil where, as I have told you, my friends and I sometimes go to paint as well. In the name of that little village, Argenteuil, you can find the word "argent," a French word that means "silver." The countless little waves made by the passing boats sparkle like silver in the sunshine.

The movement of the sails, their shapes in the water—the rowboats that seem to chase after them—the reflections and the waves, these are the things I want to paint. And to get that feeling of things moving, the clouds, the water, the people, and the boats, I use my brush to put many colors side by side, and I look for the gayest colors in my paint tubes and boxes.

I watch closely: I see a man on a dock looking at his friend who is fishing from a sailboat. Ducks and moorhens swim by, and more sailboats pass in the distance. Everybody seems to be happy to be swimming or sailing. The ladies are wearing long dresses, which are not very practical for boating but—oh, so lovely! The men wear their "boaters" when they go rowing. I, too, am happy: I have a parasol to shade me from the sun, I set up my outdoor easel and, in the broad daylight, I paint. Will I be able to put on the canvas all the impressions of light and life that I see?

For the fun of it, I looked in my childhood dictionary for the definitions and illustrations of each type of boat. Do you know them all?

SKIFF n. A light rowboat (see illustration on opposite page).

GIG n. A rowboat designed for speed, rowed by four or six oars. The gig of a yacht is for the use of the owner and his guests.

DINGHY n. 1. A rowboat used for pleasure. 2. A rowboat used as tender to a vessel.

KAYAK n. A long narrow boat for one person, that tips very easily.

To Live On the Water

My painter friends also come to paint at the water's edge. One of them, Claude Monet, who has become as famous as I am, did not want to leave the river at all; so he built a sort of hut on a little boat, which we called his "floating studio." One of our friends, Edouard Manet, did a painting of it (at right) and Charles-François Daubigny made an etching of it, too (below).

The splendor of water is just what I tried to paint in *The Skiff*: the bright yellow of the boat and the sapphire blue of the river burst before my eyes like fireworks set to music. I love to paint water, and all of my artist friends do, too. The water flowing between the river banks—serene now but constantly changing—lends my brush lightness and joy.

A Woman's Grace

For centuries, artists, inspired by the grace and beauty of the body, have painted nudes, especially women. All during my long lifetime, I often painted women swimming in rivers or at the seaside, or sometimes just drying themselves off and brushing their hair after a bath. Their skin is always so beautiful in the light—any light, daylight, sunlight, or imaginary light.

This sketch called *Stepping Out of the Bath* reveals to you what I mean. But I am equally charmed by *The Washerwomen at Cagnes*, so graceful even though they are doing very hard work on a sunny day in southern France.

Dressed in their pink and blue dresses under the parasol pines (in southern France, where I have lived for a long time), the washerwomen come to do their laundry, which they carry in baskets on their heads; they make a happy occasion of it, singing as they soak, scrub, and wring the washing. I love to watch all the people who come to the river to work, swim, row boats, and play.

The Boating Party

Friends, acquaintances, and even strangers, all gathered happily for *The Luncheon of the Boating Party*. For a long time I had wanted to paint these lovely young women and their friends, the boatmen, all enjoying a luncheon together on a summer's day, under a restaurant awning.

But the work was very long and hard; I began painting it outdoors and finished it only a year later, in my studio. The canvas was very large, and it cost a lot of money just to buy the paints to cover such a big space. It was hard work, too, and often I was tempted to leave it unfinished! But finally the painting is done. It is a happy painting; I hope you like it.

We French think that a day in the country is truly perfect only if we get together with friends at a restaurant for a good lunch. Seeing the gaiety of my friends talking, playing with their dogs, telling each other stories, made me feel like putting a canvas on the easel and painting this moment of

happiness. My wife is there—how pretty she is!—some friends, too, and, way in the back, a young girl is arranging her bonnet; or perhaps she is covering her ears to keep from hearing too much silly gossip!

Sometimes Everyone Starts to Dance

Here is an engaged couple—you can see that they love each other. She is a florist; he is a painter. She wears her prettiest dress, and he holds his top hat and invites her to dance. But she is a little shy. How do I know so much about them? Do you think these are imaginary people? Not at all, they have been my friends for a long time, and he, Alfred Sisley, is a very great painter.

Finch

Sometimes everyone starts dancing. Ah! to dance. How much I enjoyed it in my younger days. My friend Sisley loves his fiancée very much and always dances with her; they make a splendid couple, he with his dark coat and white shirt, and she with her lovely gold and red striped dress. The trees, of a green as tender as their love, are full of birds, of course, but I have not painted them; it is better to imagine them.

"She waltzed with delicious abandon in the arms of a blond fellow who looked like a boatman."

Do you remember how I introduced myself wearing a little round hat? Here it is again, or one very much like it. But I am barely thirty-five years old here, and this time I felt like painting my *Self-Portrait* in blue and beige colors. I also wanted to paint a large picture full of people in blue and light colors dancing in an outdoor garden in Montmartre. Montmartre is a pretty section of the city of Paris. It is located on a hill, with charming cobblestoned streets, colorful gardens, and friendly cafés. It is very famous because so many artists have lived and worked there, including myself.

On the postcard at the bottom of the page you can see that an artist has set up his easel right in the middle of the street—no doubt an Impressionist like me! Honoré Daumier often made fun of our strange habits. This drawing (below, right) is captioned: "The first one copies nature and the second one copies the first!"

549bis VIEUX-PARIS. - La Butte Montmartre, Cabaret du Lapin Agile (XVIIIe arr).

F. F.
PARIS

The Ball at the Moulin de la Galette

Watching people dance gives me many ideas for drawings and paintings. The pretty dresses swaying with the rapid steps of the waltzers, the bodies and the heads whirling faster and faster—they look like spinning tops, gaily spinning tops. But it's not only the people—sometimes it seems to me that even the Chinese lanterns that light the ballroom are whirling and dancing!

One day, on coming back to Montmartre from the country, I decided to paint at the Moulin de la Galette, a café near my home, where people from the neighborhood went dancing on Sundays. The owner of this open-air dance hall let me set myself up—with my easel and canvas and all my equipment—in the garden, right in the middle of the outdoor ballroom. It was a big canvas, about four feet high and six feet wide, and heavy, too.

But I needed it to paint the rhythm of the dancers, stepping more and more lightly, under the ever changing shadows of the trees and the light from the Chinese lanterns: yellow and blue and pink, and blue and pink once again, and again and again.

And so here I am, ready to paint in the garden of the Moulin de la Galette, under the twinkling lanterns, under the leafy umbrella of the trees, in the glow of the beautiful dresses and smiling faces. Here, too, black-ribboned straw boaters, casting golden reflections, appear on the heads of many of the friends that I have called together for this festival of painting and youth.

Thinking that he was making fun of my picture, a journalist wrote: "The figures dance on a ground that looks like purplish clouds darkening the sky on a stormy day." But that is exactly the effect I wanted to show!

I worked as fast as I could; my little tubes of color danced; the brushes too, swiftly, barely touching the canvas. And how happy I was in this sparkling light. Today, I know that my painting (above) has become very famous. Many people go to see it in the museum. It is called *The Ball at the Moulin de la Galette.* "Moulin" is the French word for "windmill." There are still many windmills where I live, although they no longer work, of course. The open-air café and dance hall is right at the foot of one. You can see the entrance to it in the photograph (opposite). And perhaps you have tasted a "galette" which is a kind of cake that French children like to eat.

If I remember correctly, I painted this scene (opposite) of *The Swing* in the garden of my house in Montmartre. All children like to play on swings, and in my day they also liked to play with hoops. (In my old dictionary I found a picture that shows you how to use one). "What fun!" thinks the little girl who waits her turn, holding a hoop tightly in her hands. Half-teasingly and a bit shyly, she seems to be asking me: "What on earth are you doing?" I answer by painting her into my picture; that is my way of telling her how pretty she looks in her flowered hat.

Hoops

Do children still know how to play with a hoop? Never mind; surely there is a swing in a park nearby. Look at the pretty dress with a row of blue bows which this girl is wearing. She is really too big to go on the swing anyway, but the child on the left is willing to let her have a turn. Have you noticed how the ground in this tree-lined garden is carpeted with pink, yellow, and blue spots from the light passing through the leaves? It is a very joyful effect, I think.

It is not just the leaves that let a nice light pass through. There are also umbrellas and parasols. They are a bit heavy, but women seem to like to carry them around, to open and close them, and make them twirl. What a graceful picture it makes when a pretty woman takes shelter from the rain or sun under an umbrella or parasol!

All kinds of weather are interesting to paint. On a cold day in town, everyone hurries. On one such day I stopped to sketch a woman keeping her hands warm in a fur muff (above). But what I wanted to show in *The Umbrellas* (left) was the special atmosphere of a rainy day, the damp, close air surrounding the crowds of people. It was not easy by any means. In fact, I had to redo the picture several times. Have I succeeded in showing all of the shades of blue that were in the air?

In any case, we all liked the busy crowds of passersby strolling or rushing about the streets of the city. Paris has become noisy and crowded: carts, bicycles, cabs, streetcars, and buses with one or several decks—the famous "imperials" had three! What fun it is to recapture all this liveliness by painting it. Another old friend, Camille Pissarro, a marvelous painter with a handsome beard, has painted many pictures of the comings and goings of city crowds and traffic.

Camille Pissarro likes to watch the crowds of people passing by as they make their way through the city. Here is his picture of a busy corner in the center of Paris. He painted it from a window in his room in the Grand Hotel Louvre. When you go to Paris you can still see this corner; it looks very much the same today as when Pissarro painted it. I think it is a splendid picture.

It is too cold to paint outside, so I am at home. My house in the Montmartre area of Paris is called the "Castle of the Mist." But it is not really a castle, and, fortunately, there is rarely any mist. I have a studio there very much like the one in the picture above, which belongs to my friend, Frédéric Bazille. He painted all of his friends gathered there together, myself included, but I no longer know if I can be recognized very well.

Studio Easel on Wheels

Here is a photograph of my Castle of the Mist, where I lived for many years and where my first two children, Pierre and Jean, were born. A lovely path full of flowers led from the street to the house. That is one of the most extraordinary charms of Paris—you go through a door and suddenly you feel as if you are very far away from the noise of the city.

My friend Bazille's painting, on the opposite page, *The Studio in Condamine Street*, shows a workroom that is clean and tidy, with the stretchers and finished pictures neatly stacked against the wall.

The friends assembled there look as if they were on a theater stage. But don't be fooled. My studio is not like that at all. There are paint tubes and brushes on every table, toys everywhere, and the children are always getting in everyone's way. My messiness is famous, it has even been written about in a book, as if my painting were not what mattered the most in the end!

Jean, Claude, and Gabrielle

As for children, how I loved to paint mine! Here is Gabrielle, the nanny (at right), patiently showing little wooden animals to baby Jean; and here is Claude (below), playing with tin soldiers. *The Girls at the Piano* (opposite) are attentively reading the music score. The light colors of their contrasting hair and dresses seemed splendid subjects to paint. Oh! to show the grace of their gestures and the harmony that music can bring!

Time and time again I have painted children, and always with delight.

I have always liked children, and my three sons most of all. I painted them when they were just little ones in the arms of their nanny Gabrielle, or when they were a little older, playing and even imitating me at my easel. Fair-haired and charming, they were perfect Renoir subjects. Well, today they are big, strong young men; one wants to be an actor and the other two want to make movies. Who knows if one or another of them will become as famous as I am?

Nowadays I often recall old times—I think of my strolls in the city or in the country, alone or with my friends. When we set our easels up in a field, the farmers would say hello and probably thought that we were lazy good-for-nothings to spend the whole day just painting. And when we set ourselves up to paint in the city on a street corner or on the sidewalk, children would gather around and sing and laugh. Probably they were thinking—who can tell?—that some day they would paint even finer pictures themselves. Where, I wonder, will all of my pictures go, in the years to come. And will you go to see them?

Yes?

WHERE TO SEE RENOIR

Renoir loved to paint children and wondered if they would go to see his paintings. Of course you will, but where? You will find in the following pages a few of the American, Canadian, and French museums where you can admire Renoir's works.

Renoir painted many pictures throughout his long life as an artist. His works have rightly become very popular and are found today in museums all over the world. In the United States, east and west, north and south, museums and collections in Boston, New York, Philadelphia, Washington, Chicago, Houston, and San Francisco (the list could go on and on!) are proud to display on their walls one or more of Renoir's beautiful paintings. Works also are found in Canada in Ottawa, Montreal, and Toronto. Why not take your parents on a visit to the art museum—there may very well be an example of Renoir's work not far from where you live.

New York, New York
The Metropolitan Museum of Art

The Metropolitan Museum of Art in New York City, for example, possesses one of the finest collections of Renoir's and other French Impressionists' paintings that exists outside their native France. The Metropolitan Museum is enormous, so big in fact that the museum guards still discover rooms of art that even *they* didn't know existed, or so they say.

In the Metropolitan, there is another version of the *Girls at the Piano* that you have already seen on page 43. See if you can spot the differences in the two paintings' colors and form.

The fluffy Newfoundland dog shown on page 45 (his name is Porto by the way) is lying at the feet of *Madame Georges Charpentier and Her Children Georgette and Paul,* a wonderful family portrait that you can see in the Metropolitan, too. Besides these portraits, the Metropolitan's collection boasts landscapes and seascapes, still lifes and bathers, examples of every type of painting that Renoir ever enjoyed practicing.

Washington, D. C.
The National Gallery of Art

The happy, carefree young women and men in the *Luncheon of the*

Boating Party (you've seen them on pages 26 and 27) are still gathered around the table, chatting and flirting in the Phillips Collection in Washington, D.C. Also in Washington, in the National Gallery of Art, you can see for yourself Renoir's wife, Aline, and the *Oarsmen at Chatou* with their little skiff bobbing along the banks of the river Seine. In the same museum you will find Renoir's view of bustling nineteenth-century Paris and the *Pont-Neuf,* which means the "new bridge" in French and is, strangely enough, the oldest bridge in Paris, spanning the Seine farther upstream from Chatou. The National Gallery of Art has as well a portrait that Renoir painted of the first wife of his friend and fellow Impressionist Claude Monet, *Camille Monet and Her Son Jean.*

Chicago, Illinois
The Art Institute of Chicago

You will find some of Renoir's favorite elements in composing a scene, the banks of the Seine, boaters, and a luncheon, in the Art Institute of Chicago's *The Rowers' Lunch*. Or if you prefer, there is a

lovely *Lady at the Piano.* Look and listen closely because Renoir's colors vibrate here with the sound of the lady's playing.

Other North American Institutions

In Houston, Texas, at the Museum of Fine Arts, you can see a splendid *Still Life with a Bouquet* that represents a bunch of bright red and yellow rose buds lying on a table next to a Japanese fan in a vase. What a good eye Renoir had for balancing one color with another! A portrait Renoir executed of *Madame Clémentine Stora* hangs in the Fine Arts Museum of San Francisco, California. He dressed her up in the traditional costume of an Algerian woman, perhaps because she was the wife of a dealer in antiques and oriental rugs. Finally, the portrait of *Gabrielle and Jean,* shown on page 42, can be seen in the National Gallery of Canada at Ottawa.

It is not surprising that many of this French painter's works have remained in France. If one day you have the chance to visit France (maybe you want to be a painter too!), here are the names of a few museums where you are sure to find excellent examples of Renoir's work.

Paris, France
Musée d'Orsay

The Musée d'Orsay rises in the center of Paris along the Seine. This museum has had an amusing history because it was first built as a great, luxurious train terminal for the Universal Exposition of 1900. One painter at the time exclaimed that the station was superb and looked like a fine arts museum. Many years later his premonition has come true and the d'Orsay's tracks, timetables, and trains have been replaced by a great number of works of art, including magnificent paintings by Renoir and his friends.

Musée de l'Orangerie
and Musée Marmottan

The Musée de l'Orangerie, also in Paris, has a modest but very good collection of 146 paintings, of which 24 are by Renoir. A number of portraits Renoir painted of Claude Monet are hanging next to many of his friend's own works in the Musée Marmottan in Paris.

Cagnes-sur-Mer, France
Les Collettes

And if you can visit the south of France near Cannes, at Cagnes-sur-Mer, you will see Renoir's house, Les Collettes, which is now a memorial museum. This is the house that Renoir had built and where he lived until his death. Despite the absence of paintings by Renoir, the house has kept the Renoir charm, especially the garden with its olive trees.

And now, it's your turn to see if other museums have paintings by Renoir. Try and hunt them down.

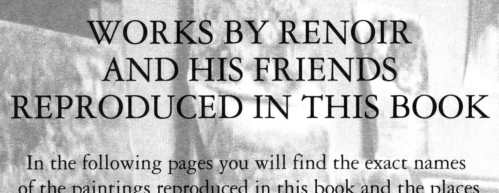

WORKS BY RENOIR
AND HIS FRIENDS
REPRODUCED IN THIS BOOK

In the following pages you will find the exact names
of the paintings reproduced in this book and the places
where they are to be found. They are listed in the order of
the pages on which they appear. Renoir's works are
mentioned by their titles and, unless otherwise specified,
all works are oil on canvas. A work's dimensions are given
in inches and centimeters, first by height, then width.

Cover and page 44
◄ *Girls at the Edge of the Sea,* 1894. 21½ x 18" (55 x 46 cm.). Durand-Ruel Collection, Paris, France and New York, New York.

Page 4
◄ *Self-portrait,* 1899(?). 16¼ x 13" (41 x 33 cm.). Sterling and Francine Clark Institute, Williamstown, Massachusetts.

Page 5
See page 20

Page 6
A sculptured and gilt wooden frame, Musée d'Orsay, Paris France. Renoir liked this Louis XV style of frame for his canvases.

Page 6, within the frame
◄ *The Parisian* (detail), 1874. National Museum of Wales, Cardiff.

Page 7
◄ *Picking Fruit,* about 1883–1886. Watercolor, gouache, and black lead pencil marks, lightly varnished, 13 x 11¾" (33 x 30 cm.). Cabinet des Dessins, Louvre, Paris, France.

Page 8
Art materials.
Illustrations taken from the *Catalogue de la Maison de couleurs Gustave Sennelier,* April 1895, Paris, France.

Page 8, lower right
The back of a neoclassical style frame. The frame backing a canvas is called a *stretcher* and is made up of four lengths of wood that are mitered (that is, cut at equally divided angles) at the joints and held in place by a wedge at each corner. Taken from *Cadres de peintres* by Isabelle Cahn.

Page 9
Pierre-Auguste Renoir, as a young man, about 1860. Photograph by A. Lefevre, about 1860. Bibliothèque Nationale, Paris, France.

Page 10

Claude Monet (1840–1928): *Impression, Sunrise,* 1872. 18½ x 25¼" (47 x 64 cm.). Musée Marmottan, Paris, France.

Page 10

Honoré Daumier (1808–1879): *Les Bons Bourgeois* (Good Middle-Class Folks). Caption: "Come, come, my dear, I assure you that this gentleman is drawing a landscape . . . you are, Sir, drawing a landscape, are you not? . . .", 1846. Lithograph. Cabinet des Dessins, Bibliothèque Nationale, Paris, France.

Page 11

The Dressmaker, about 1879. Pencil, 16½ x 10¾" (42 x 27.5 cm.). Mr. and Mrs. Paul Mellon Collection, Upperville, Virginia.

Young Woman Reading an Illustrated Magazine, about 1880–1881. 18⅛ x 22" (46 x 56 cm.). Museum of Art, Rhode Island School of Design, Providence, Rhode Island.

Pages 12-13

Charles-François Daubigny (1817–1878): Maisons-Laffitte. Illustration taken from Jules Janin's *Guide du voyageur de Paris à la mer (Traveler's Guide from Paris to the Sea),* 1862. Bibliothèque historique de la Ville de Paris, France.

Page 14

Dictionary illustration: *Petit Larousse illustré.*

Page 14

The Seine at Argenteuil, 1874. 20⅛ x 25⅝" (57 x 65 cm.). Portland Art Museum, Portland, Oregon.

Page 15

The Boaters' Dance Hall, Bougival. Photograph dating from the nineteenth century. Bibliothèque Nationale, Paris, France.

Page 16

Claude Monet (1840–1928): *The River* (detail), 1868. The Art Institute of Chicago, Chicago, Illinois.

Page 28

The Painter Sisley and His Wife, about 1868. 41¾ x 29⅛" (106 x 74 cm.). Wallraf-Richartz Museum, Cologne, Germany.

Finch, see page 14.

Page 29

Dancing Couple, 1883. Pen and ink, 15¼ x 7¼" (38.6 x 18.6 cm.). Henry P. McIlhenny Philadelphia, Pennsylvania.

Page 30

Self-portrait, about 1876. 28¾ x 22" (73 x 56 cm.). Fogg Art Museum, Harvard University, Cambridge, Massachusetts.

Page 31

Honoré Daumier (1808–1879): The Landscape Artists, lithograph from the Album *The Artists,* published in *Le Charivari,* May 12, 1865. Staatsgalerie, Stuttgart, Germany.

Below, Vieux-Paris, La Butte Montmartre. Cabaret du Lapin Agile. Nineteenth-century photograph.

Pages 32–33 (details) and page 34

The Ball at the Moulin de la Galette, 1876. 51⅝ x 68⅞" (131 x 175 cm.). Musée d'Orsay, Paris, France.

Page 35

Entrance to the gardens of the Moulin de la Galette. Nineteenth-century photograph.

Page 36

The Swing, 1876. 35¾ x 28" (92 x 73 cm.). Musée d'Orsay, Paris, France.

Page 37

Hoops, see page 14.
Detail, see page 38.

Page 38

The Umbrellas, about 1881–1885. 70⅞ x 45¼" (180 x 115 cm.). National Gallery, London, England.

Woman with a Muff, about 1883. Pastel and red chalk, 20¾ x 14¼" (52.7 x 36.2 cm.). The Metropolitan Museum of Art, New York, New York.

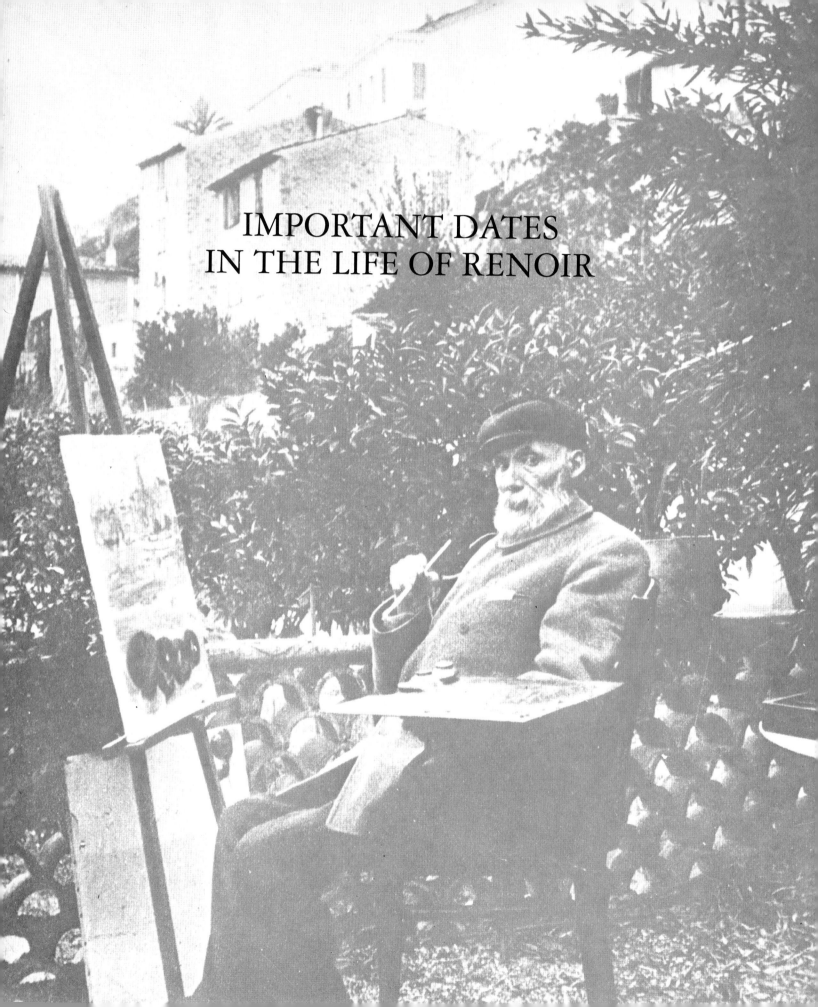

IMPORTANT DATES
IN THE LIFE OF RENOIR

1841   Pierre-Auguste Renoir is born on February 25 in Limoges, France.

1845   The Renoir family moves to Paris.

1854   He works as a decorator of china and porcelain. A few years later, he also paints fans and window blinds.

1862   He enters the Ecole des Beaux Arts, the Fine Arts Academy of Paris. Meets Claude Monet, Alfred Sisley and Frédéric Bazille.

1866   Becomes friendly with Camille Pissarro and other painters in a group led by Edouard Manet that meets often in the Café Guerbois in Paris.

1867   His paintings are refused by the Salon, the important official art exhibition that is held each year in Paris. Acceptance in the Salon, which is run by the professors at the Ecole des Beaux-Arts, is much desired as it is considered a seal of approval for the work of talented young artists. Bazille offers to let him paint in his studio on Condamine Street.

1868   The Salon accepts one of his paintings.

1869   He works with Monet at La Grenouillère.

1870   War breaks out, and he enlists in the cavalry in Bordeaux.

1871   He returns to Paris.

1873   Renoir meets the important Paris art dealer, M. Durand-Ruel, who becomes a faithful admirer of his art.

1874   First group show where people speak of "Impressionist" painting. The exhibition is held in the gallery of the photographer Nadar.

1876   Second Impressionist exhibition. Renoir takes part in all the Impressionist exhibitions thereafter (1877, 1879, 1880, 1881, 1882) except the last one (1886). He meets the art publisher Charpentier.

1879   At the Salon, his painting, *Mme. Charpentier and her Children,* is a great success.

1881   Travels in Algeria, then goes to Italy to see the paintings of Raphael. Also visits Florence, Venice, Rome, Naples and Pompeii.

1882   Returns from Italy and goes to visit Paul Cézanne at Estaque in the south of France, where they paint together. Over the years, his visits with Cézanne become more and more frequent.

1883   First one-man show of his work is organized by M. Durand-Ruel.

1885   His first son, Pierre, is born.

1888–   He makes more trips to the south of France, as well as to Spain
1892   and Normandy. For the first time, the French government buys one of his paintings.

1894   His second son, Jean, is born. The Renoirs are living in the Castle of the Mist in the Montmartre section of Paris.

1898   Renoir suffers an acute attack of rheumatism. He becomes more and more seriously ill.

1901   Birth of his third son, Claude (nicknamed "Coco").

1902   Moves to Cannet, a few miles from Cannes in southern France.

1905– Settles in Cagnes and buys a tract of land called "Les Collettes"
1909   where he builds a house.

1910   Takes a trip to Munich, Germany. Writes the preface to *A
       Treatise on Painting* by Cennino Cennini, an early fifteenth-
       century Italian author.

1914– Pierre and Jean are both seriously wounded in World War I.
1915   His wife Aline dies.

1919   Visits the Louvre Museum in Paris, where he sees several of his
       paintings hung. Death of Renoir on December 3.

First published in the United States of America in 1991 by
Rizzoli International Publications, Inc.
300 Park Avenue South, New York, New York 10010

Library of Congress Cataloging-in-Publication Data

Skira-Venturi, Rosabianca.
    [Dimanche avec Renoir. English]
    A weekend with Renoir / by Rosabianca Skira-Venturi
        p.   cm.
    Translation of: Un dimanche avec Renoir.
    Summary: The nineteenth-century artist talks about his life and
work as if entertaining the reader for a weekend.
    ISBN 0-8478-1438-6
    1. Renoir, Auguste. 1841–1919—Juvenile literature.   2. Painter–
France–Biography–Juvenile literature.   [1. Renoir, Auguste,
1841–1919.   2. Artists.]   I. Title.   II. Title: Renoir.
ND553.R45S4813   1991
759.4—dc20   91-12426
                                                                      CIP
                                                                       AC

Design by Mary McBride

Printed in Great Britain